DATE DU

Distinctions in Nature

Flowering and Nonflowering Plants Explained

Laura L. Sullivan

Cavendish Square

New York

Published in 2017 by Cavendish Square Publishing, LLC
243 5th Avenue, Suite 136, New York, NY 10016

Library of Congress Cataloging-in-Publication Data

Names: Sullivan, Laura L.
Title: Flowering and nonflowering plants explained / Laura L. Sullivan.
Description: New York : Cavendish Square, 2017. | Series: Distinctions in nature | Includes index.
Identifiers: ISBN 9781502621771 (pbk.) | ISBN 9781502621795 (library bound) |
ISBN 9781502621788 (6 pack) | ISBN 9781502621801 (ebook)
Subjects: LCSH: Plants–Juvenile literature. | Angiosperms–Juvenile literature. | Cryptogams–Juvenile literature.
Classification: LCC QK49.S85 2017 | DDC 580–dc23

Editorial Director: David McNamara
Editor: Fletcher Doyle
Copy Editor: Nathan Heidelberger
Associate Art Director: Amy Greenan
Designer: Stephanie Flecha
Production Coordinator: Karol Szymczuk
Photo Research: J8 Media

Printed in the United States of America

Contents

Plants grow almost everywhere in the world. They thrive in hot, wet places like this rain forest.

Introduction: How Plants Spread

Plants grow almost everywhere. A few kinds even grow in Antarctica, the coldest continent. Plants are so abundant because they have adapted to many environments. Some can grow in the deep shade of a rain forest. Others can survive in deserts.

All plants have things in common. They are living things that grow in the earth. They absorb water and nutrients from the soil. Plants make energy from the sun using **photosynthesis**. They produce the oxygen we need to survive.

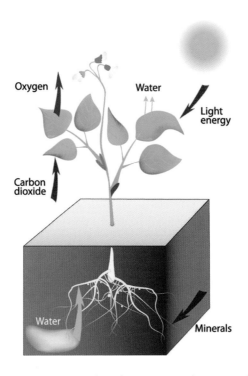

Oxygen

Water

Light
energy

Carbon
dioxide

Water

Minerals

Plants use photosynthesis to make the energy they need to grow.

One of the biggest differences among plants is the way they **reproduce**. Most plants that you see make **flowers**. These plants are called **angiosperms**. Some flowers are big and colorful, like a rose or a hibiscus. Other flowers are so tiny that you might not even notice them. The flowers play an important role in reproduction. They allow flowering plants to make seeds.

Flowering plants are the most common of all plants.

Other plants, however, don't have flowers. There are several kinds of nonflowering plants. Some, like **conifers**, still make seeds. They make them inside of cones instead of flowers. Conifers are **gymnosperms**. Other kinds of plants don't make seeds at all. Ferns and mosses make **spores**. Spores are very tiny—they are usually only one cell.

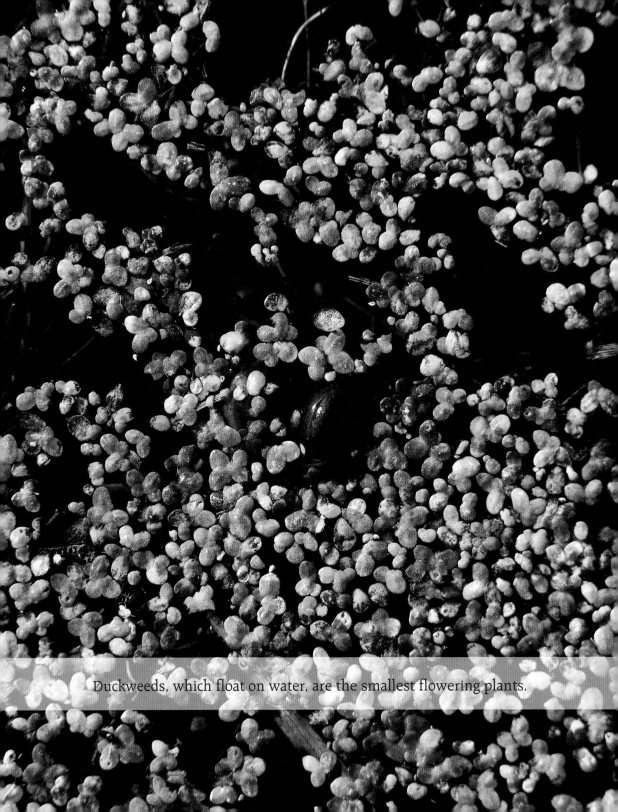

Duckweeds, which float on water, are the smallest flowering plants.

1 Flowering and Nonflowering Plants All Around

No matter where you are right now, there is probably a flowering plant nearby. You might not realize it because they don't have flowers all the time. You might not even recognize some of them as flowers. The smallest is the size of two grains of sand. The tallest flower (the corpse flower) is more than 10 feet (3 meters) tall. Grasses are flowering plants. So are most plants you have in your garden, and many trees.

But some of the plants around you don't ever make flowers. The group of trees known as conifers are all nonflowering.

Conifers make seeds, but they don't have flowers or fruit.

Conifers include pine, fir, spruce, redwoods, and cypress. Christmas trees are conifers.

Ferns are another kind of nonflowering plant. Like other plants, they have roots, stems, and leaves. Their leaves are called fronds, and they grow in a tightly curled spiral called a **fiddlehead** that later opens. Spores are released from the underside of the frond. These spores are so tiny that they can be spread by the wind.

Mosses are also nonflowering plants. They are small, soft plants that usually grow in clumps. Most are just 1 or 2 inches (2.5 or 5 centimeters) tall. Their roots can attach to rocks.

Zoom In

Flowering plants yield fruits and vegetables. A few nonflowering plants may also be eaten. Pine nuts come from nonflowering pine trees. Some ferns are safe to eat.

Ferns are another kind of plant that doesn't make flowers.

The earliest plants in the age of dinosaurs didn't have flowers.

2 Flower's Power

magine a lush prehistoric forest of ferns, some the size of modern trees. Dragonflies as big as hawks soar overhead. Giant roaches crawl along the forest floor. Millions of years later, huge dinosaurs munch on towering conifers. These earliest ancient plants were all nonflowering. To reproduce, they either made spores or had seeds inside of cones.

Then, about 125 million years ago, the first flowering plants **evolved**. It wasn't long before they took over the plant kingdom.

Flowering plants are very adaptable and can grow in many environments. This tussock grass grows in parts of Antarctica.

Today, flowering plants outnumber nonflowering plants twenty to one. Why are flowering plants so successful?

One reason is that they have adapted to more environments than nonflowering plants. Another is that they mature faster. But the main reasons have to do with **pollen** dispersal and fruit. Compared with nonflowering plants like conifers, flowering plants have reproductive advantages.

Pollen consists of microscopic grains that carry a plant's genetic material. Pollen is the male part of

Plants use tiny grains of pollen to reproduce.

the reproductive process. Conifers release their pollen to the wind. They depend on luck to spread the pollen to the female part of the tree. After **fertilization**, seeds develop in the cones. The cones offer some protection to the seeds.

Most conifers have both male and female parts on the same tree. So when the wind blows the pollen, the tree often fertilizes itself. The seeds that result only get material from the parent plant. Sometimes the wind will blow pollen to another tree. Then the seed (and baby tree) has the qualities of both parent trees.

Having two parents provides genetic diversity. This will give the offspring differences that might help them survive. While this sometimes happens by luck in wind-pollinated conifers, flowering plants don't need to rely on luck.

Most conifers rely on the wind to spread their pollen.

Most flowering plants use insects, birds, and bats to spread their pollen. Plants can't travel, so when they use animals to help them, the pollen can spread much farther. Plants that grow very far apart can share genetic material and make seeds.

Flowers have sweet nectar to attract creatures such as bees and butterflies. While they drink, the pollen attaches to them. There are both male and female parts in each flower. When the animal moves to another flower, the pollen transfers to the female part. Then, a seed can develop.

Most flowering plants use bees, butterflies, bats, or other animals to help spread their pollen.

Flowers have evolved in plants that are specially designed to attract pollinators. Some petals have colors that are very attractive to bees. Some have even developed strange shapes to bring in pollinators. Some orchids look or even smell like insects. They lure insects in search of a mate.

Another difference between flowering and nonflowering plants can be found in the seeds. Conifer seeds are bare and exposed. Flowering plants, however, develop a fleshy coating over their seeds. This is the

Some flowers, such as this fly orchid, evolved to look like insects to lure pollinators.

Flowering and Nonflowering Plants Explained

Zoom In

Flower smells can attract pollinators. Some flies lay their eggs on dead animals. The corpse flower, which smells like rotting meat, lures hundreds of flies. These flies are tricked into pollinating the corpse flower.

fruit. Animals think most fruit is delicious. They help spread the seeds when they carry the fruit away to eat. Sometimes they eat the fruit and leave the seeds. Other times, they swallow the seeds, too. Seeds can pass through the digestive system and still be able to grow after they come out in the feces.

1. Animals get nutrition from fruit, which contains seeds.

2. The key to fern reproduction is on the underside of their fronds.

3 Be a Plant Detective

One of the main distinctions between flowering and nonflowering plants is the way they reproduce. Review the traits of the plants in each question and apply what you have read to your answers.

1. In flowering plants, the seeds are inside the fruit. How does it help the plant if animals eat the fruit?
2. A fern doesn't have flowers or cones, or even seeds. How does it reproduce?

3. Butterflies often visit coneflowers and other flowering plants.

4. Squirrels find tasty treats inside of pine cones that they gather.

3. You see a bush covered in brightly colored flowers. As you get closer, you notice that the flowers smell sweet. How does the sweet smell help to spread its pollen?

4. You see a tall tree with cones on it. Is it a flowering or a nonflowering plant? Why?

1. Animals will move the seeds to different places when they eat the fruit and the seeds pass through their digestive system. This expands the places where the plants grow.

2. Ferns make tiny spores instead of seeds. They are carried on the wind.

3. Flowers have bright colors and sweet scents that tell bees, flies, butterflies, and other insects that there is nectar in the flowers. When the insects look for nectar, they pick up pollen that they spread to other flowers. Flowers make seeds and fruit when insects bring them pollen.

4. It is a nonflowering plant. Conifers grow their seeds in cones instead of in flowers.

Even though cycads are nonflowering plants, they need insects to help them pollinate.

4 8 Rule Breakers

There are a few plants that break— or seem to break—the rules about flowering and nonflowering plants. Most nonflowering plants spread their pollen or spores with the wind. However, cycads— nonflowering plants that look like a cross between a palm and a fern—rely on beetles for pollination.

The yew is a conifer that seems like an exception. Only flowering plants make fruit, but the yew makes a special kind of cone that is almost like a fruit. Although the rest of the yew is very poisonous, the fruit is sweet.

Although it is a conifer, the yew makes a fruit-like structure around its seeds.

Oak and pine trees can make so much pollen that gets wind-blown that cars can become covered with it.

Plants that are wind pollinated, like corn, are often planted close together.

Many birds like to eat yew "fruits." Then the seeds fall to the earth to grow a new yew tree.

Even though most flowering plants rely on animals for pollination, some use wind, like most nonflowering plants do. Usually these plants have very tiny green flowers that don't have petals. Some common examples include corn, oak trees, and many grasses.

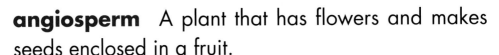

angiosperm A plant that has flowers and makes seeds enclosed in a fruit.

conifers The group of trees that produces cones and generally has evergreen, needlelike leaves.

evolve To change slowly through succeeding generations by means of random mutations.

fertilization To create offspring through the joining of male and female genetic material.

fiddlehead The furled frond of a young fern.

flower The seed-bearing part of a plant, often showy and brightly colored.

fruit The fleshy, sweet part of a plant that surrounds the seeds.

gymnosperm A plant that produces seeds that are not enclosed in a fruit.

photosynthesis The process by which green plants use sunlight to make energy.

pollen A fine, powder-like substance produced by the male part of a flower.

reproduce To create children or offspring.

spore A one-celled reproductive part of a fern, moss, or fungus.

Find Out More

Books

Aston, Dianna. *A Seed Is Sleepy.* San Francisco, CA: Chronicle, 2014.

Ingoglia, Gina. *The Tree Book for Kids and Their Grown-Ups.* New York: Brooklyn Botanic Garden, 2013.

Macken, JoAnn Early. *Flip, Float, Fly! Seeds on the Move.* New York: Holiday House, 2008.

Worth, Bonnie. *Oh Say Can You Seed? All About Flowering Plants.* New York: Random House, 2001.

Websites

Biology 4 Kids—Angiosperms
http://www.biology4kids.com/files/plants_
angiosperm.html
This page has information on angiosperms (flowering plants) as well as links to pages about gymnosperms, ferns, mosses, and other topics about plants.

Ducksters: Flowering Plants
http://www.ducksters.com/science/biology/
flowering_plants.php
Ducksters has facts and easy-to-understand diagrams about the life cycle and reproduction of flowering plants.

Real Trees 4 Kids—Conifers
http://www.realtrees4kids.org/threefive/conifers.htm
This site, about trees and tree farming, explains some of the main characteristics of conifers, or cone-bearing trees.

Index

Page numbers in **boldface** are illustrations.

Laura L. Sullivan is the author of more than thirty fiction and nonfiction books for children, including the fantasies *Under the Green Hill* and *Guardian of the Green Hill*. She has written many books for Cavendish Square, including three titles in the Distinctions in Nature series.